Wyoming, 2018

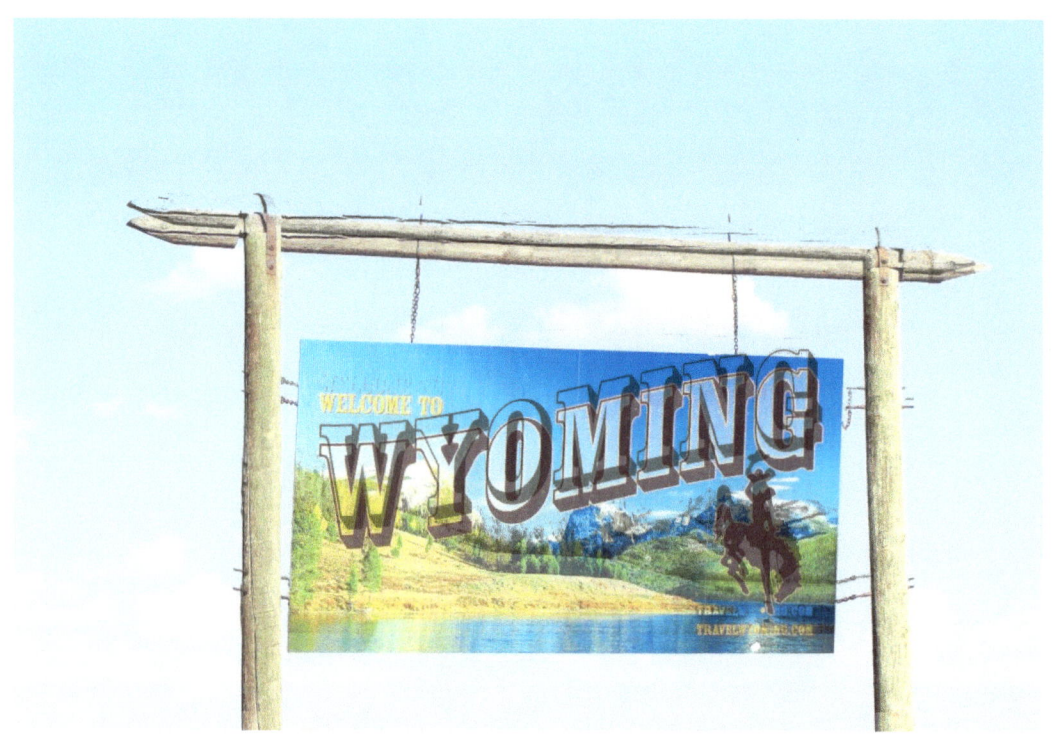

WYOMING mode
i LOVE the road

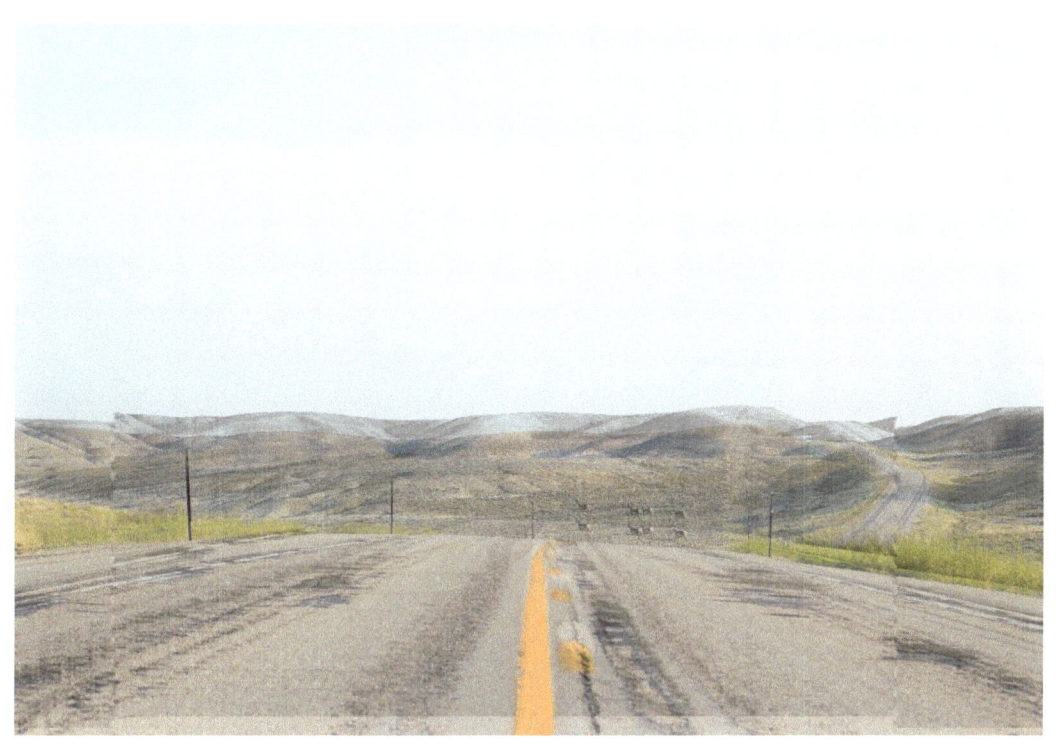

"THERE'S A CHANCE FOR EVERYBODY, YOU KNOW"

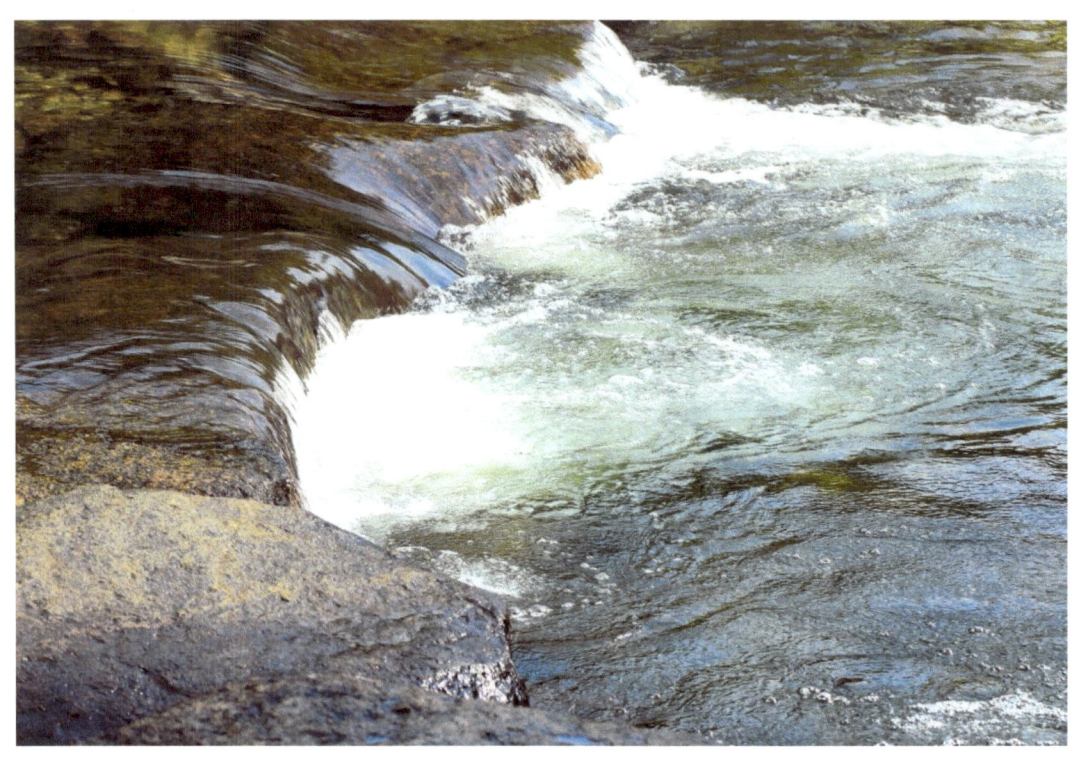

it's CLEAR here

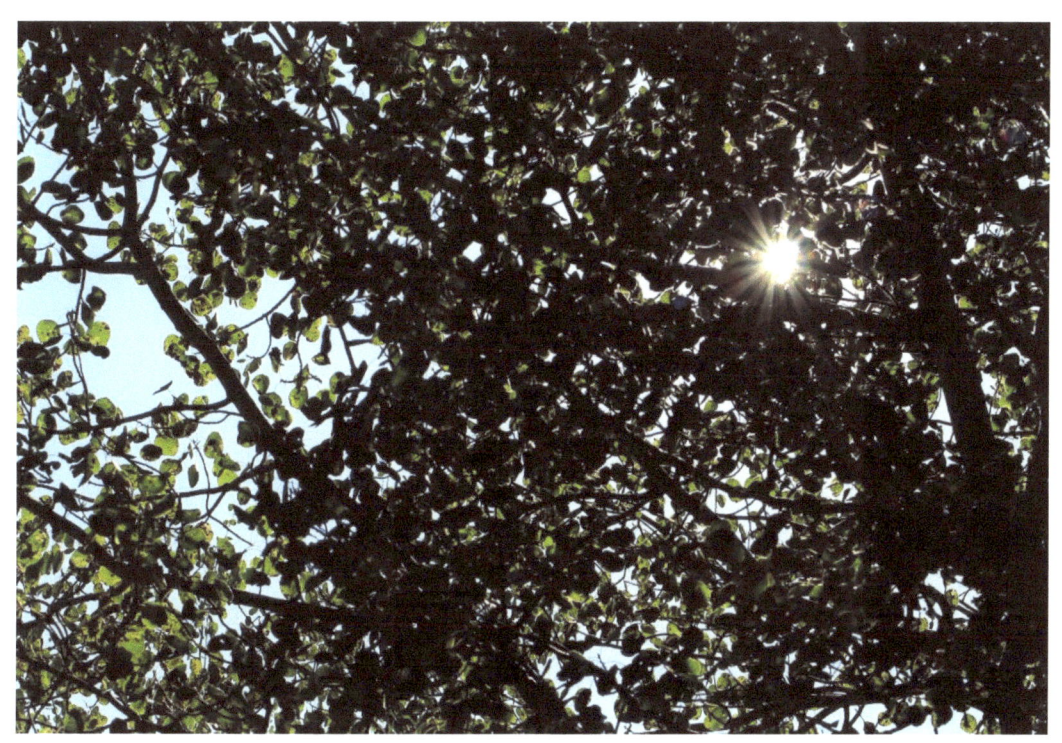

it's CLEAR here
edition 2

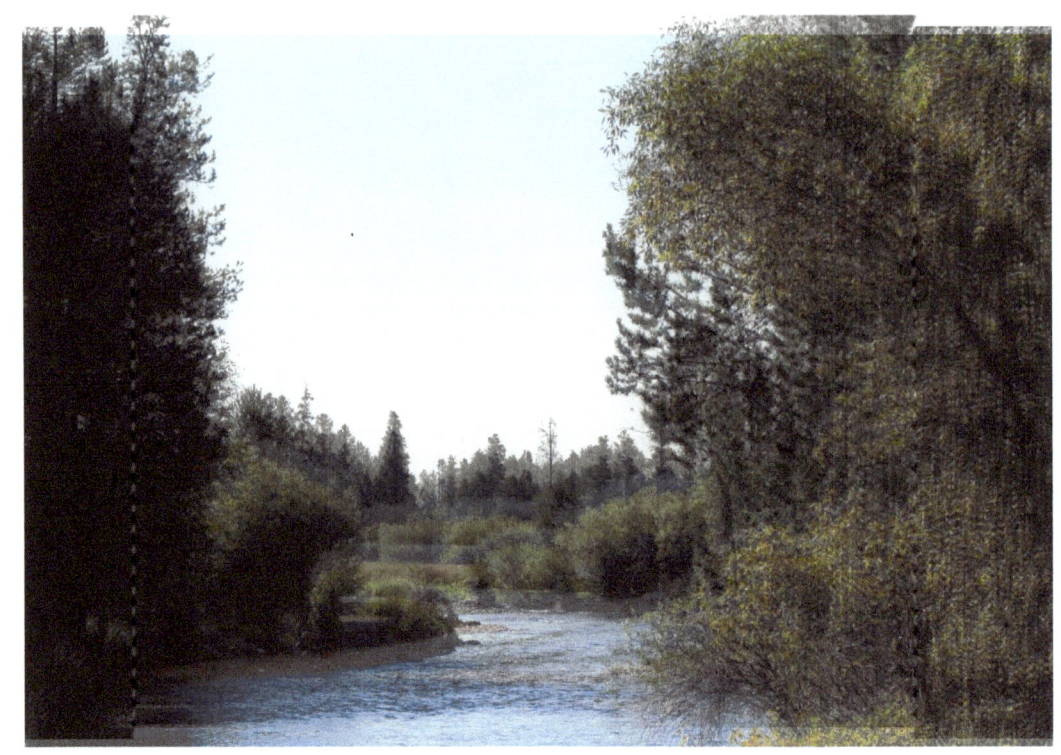

so much to explore
WYOMING, i adore

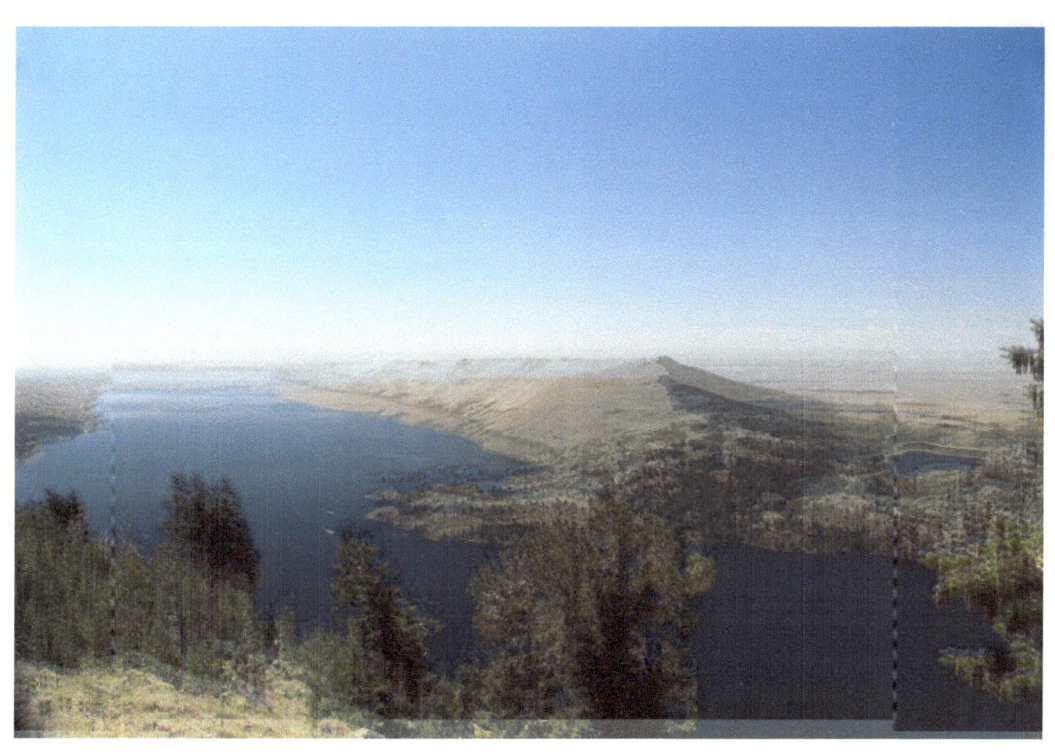

I want to be a l i v e through it all
i WANT to be alive with AWE

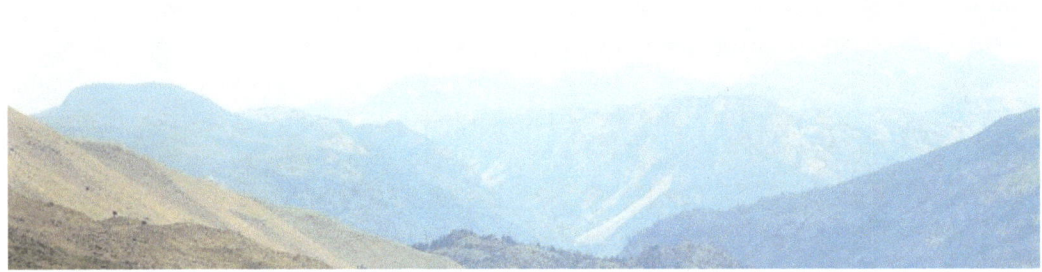

WYOMING spoke to me in silence
wyoming SPOKE guidance

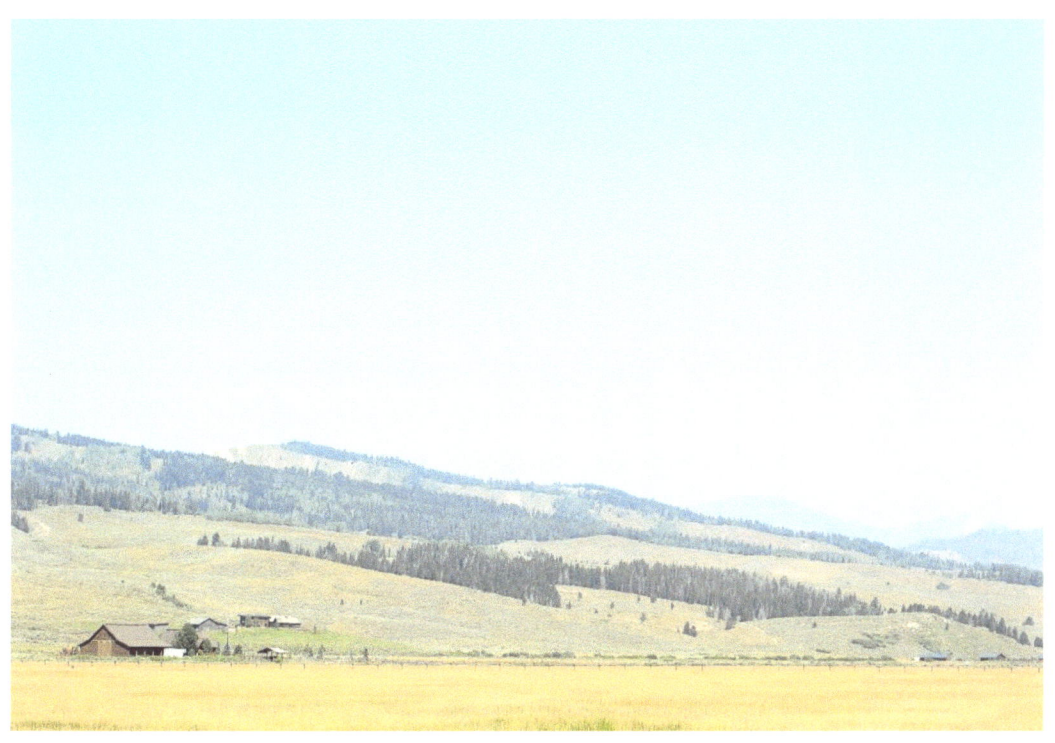

SO much to explore
WYOMING, i adore
edition 2

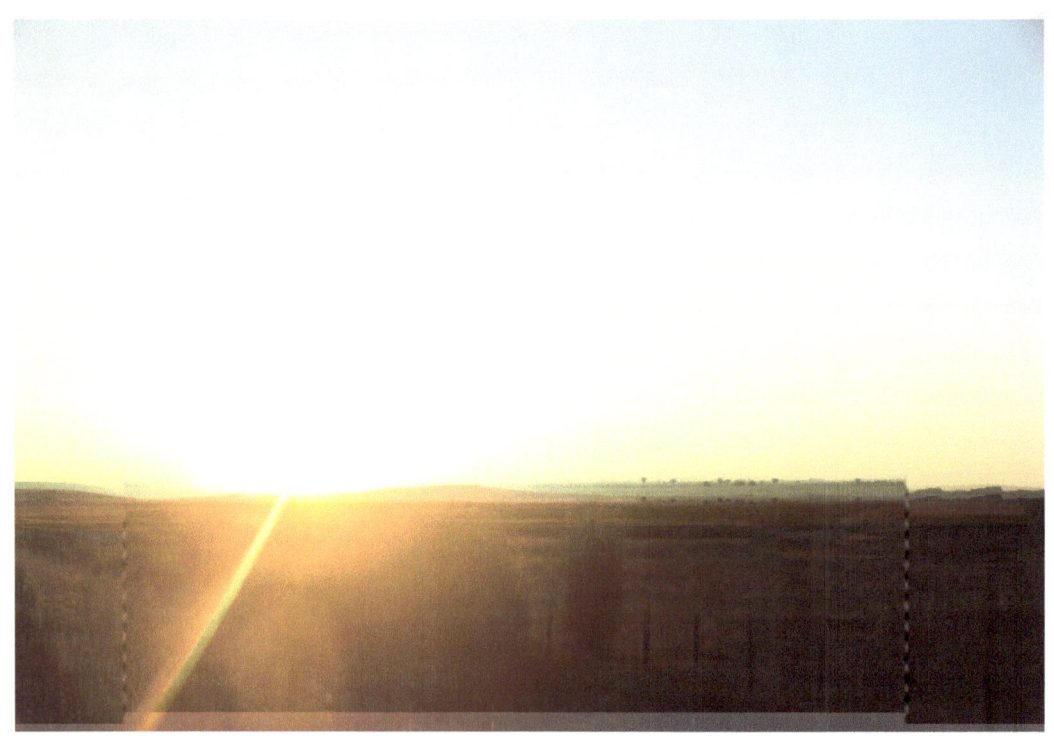

never part from ART
give it your HEART

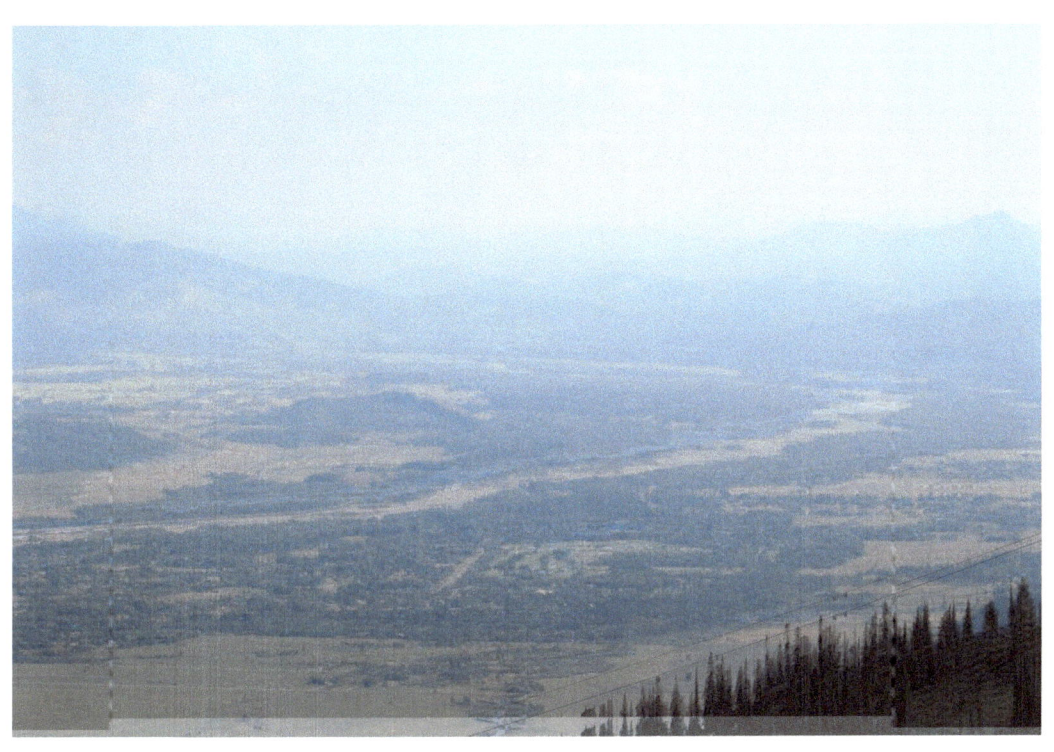

TRAVEL to evolve
evolve to TRAVEL

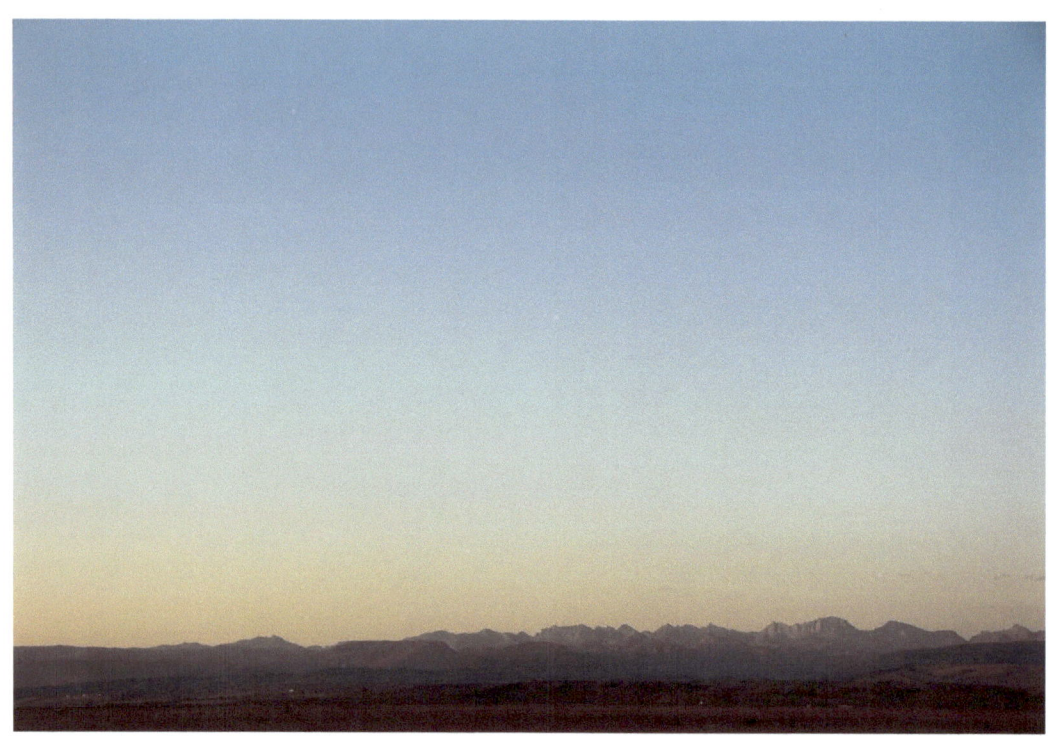

never part from ART
give it your HEART
edition 2

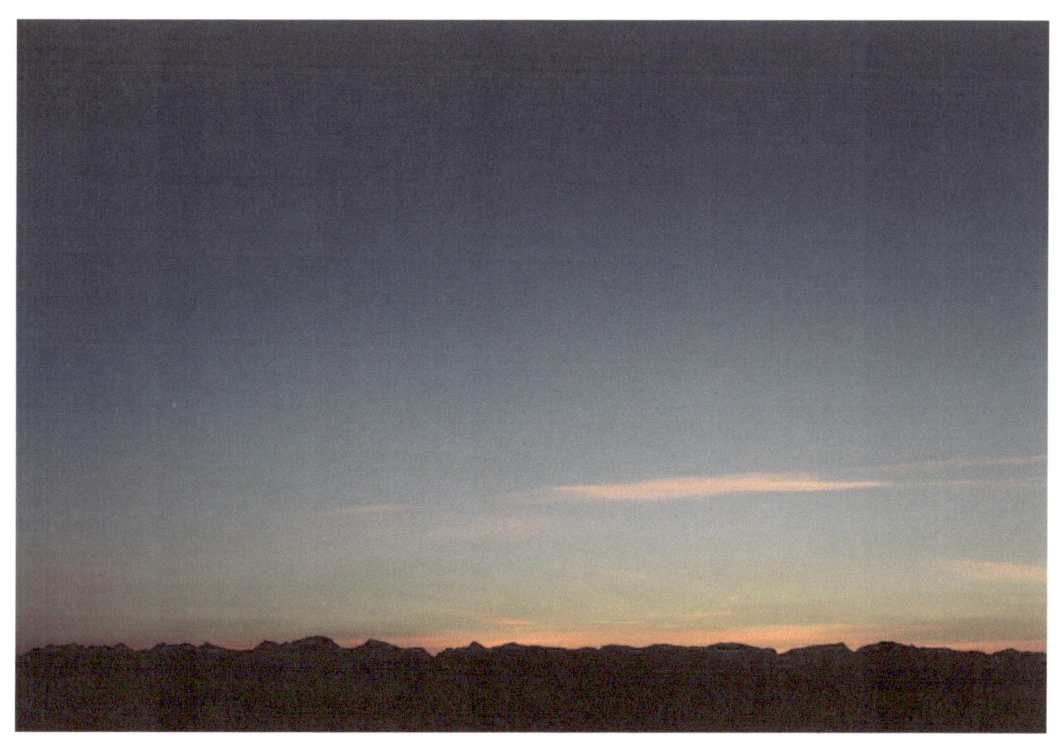

WYOMING is a w h o l e new story
l o v e its beauty and its GLORY

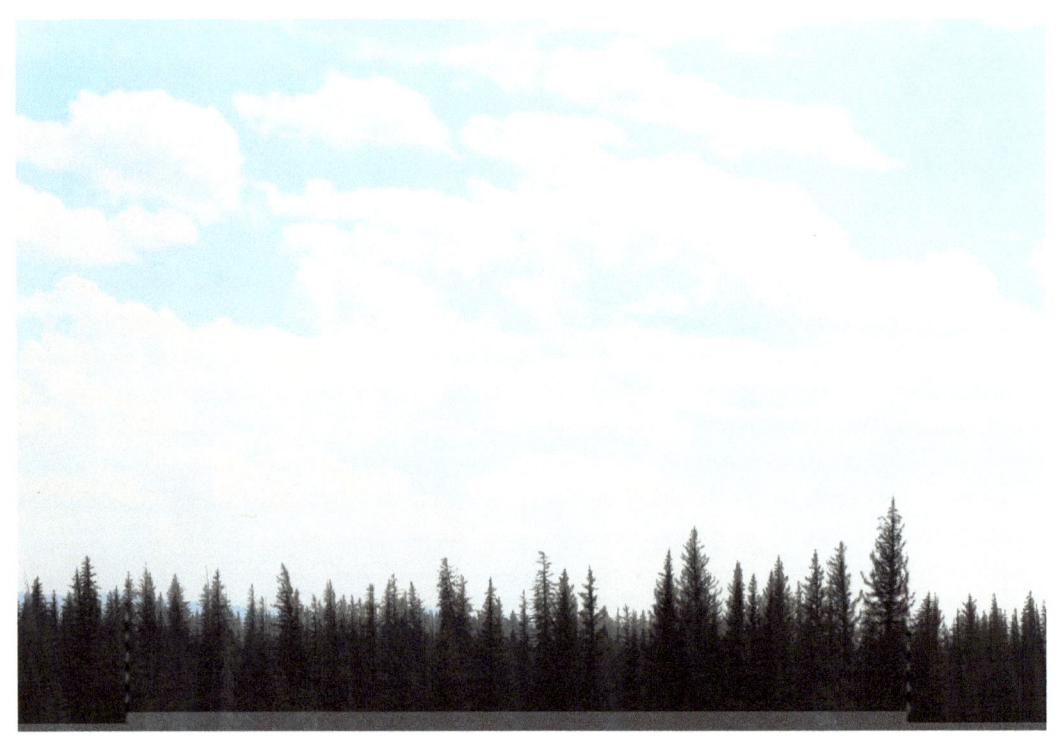

HIGH off the VIEWS
and that's the truth

sO hard to say goodbye to views so HIgh

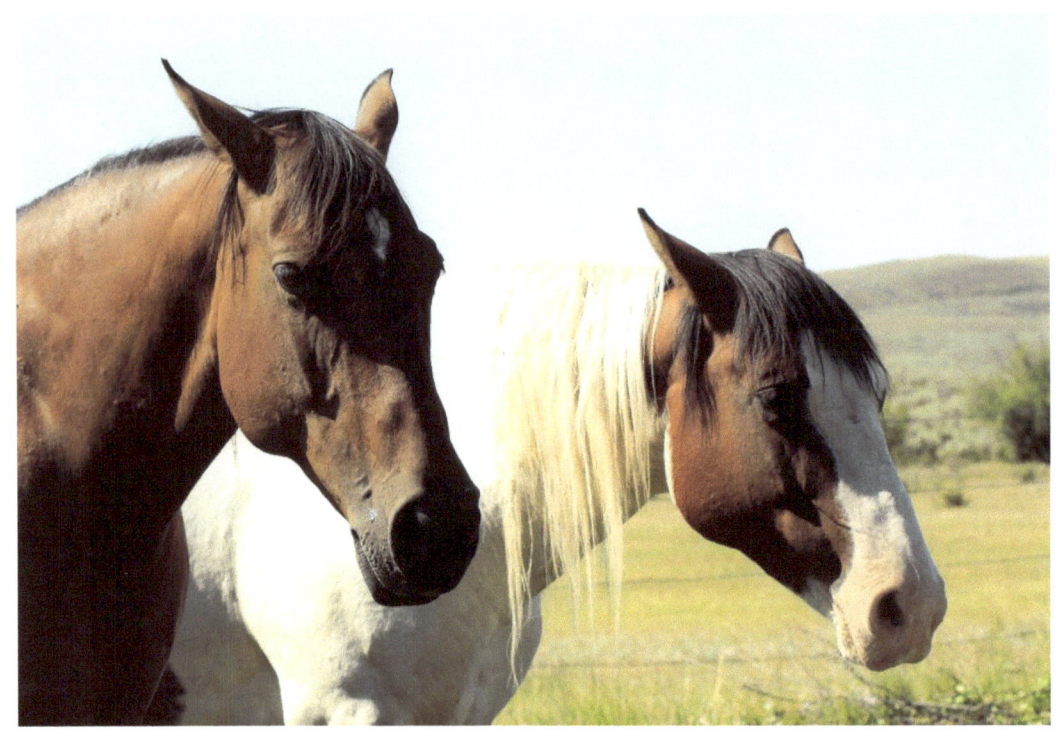

away from the california fence
WYOMING made SENSE

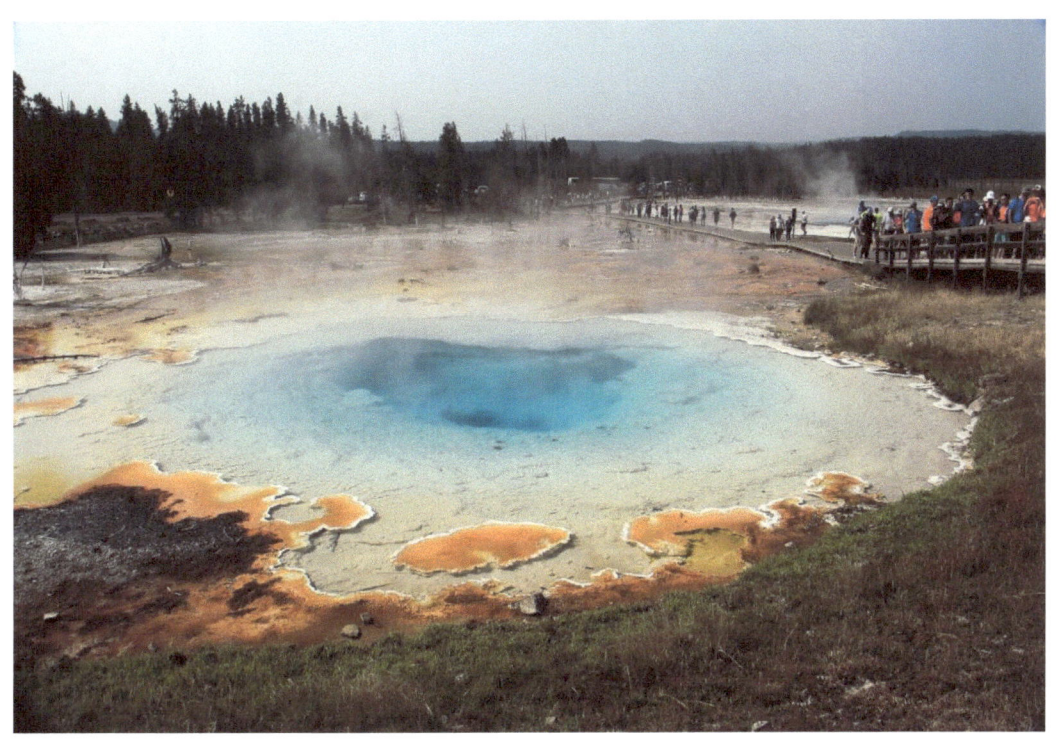

i REMEMBER it clearly
WYOMING is b e a u t i f u l yearly

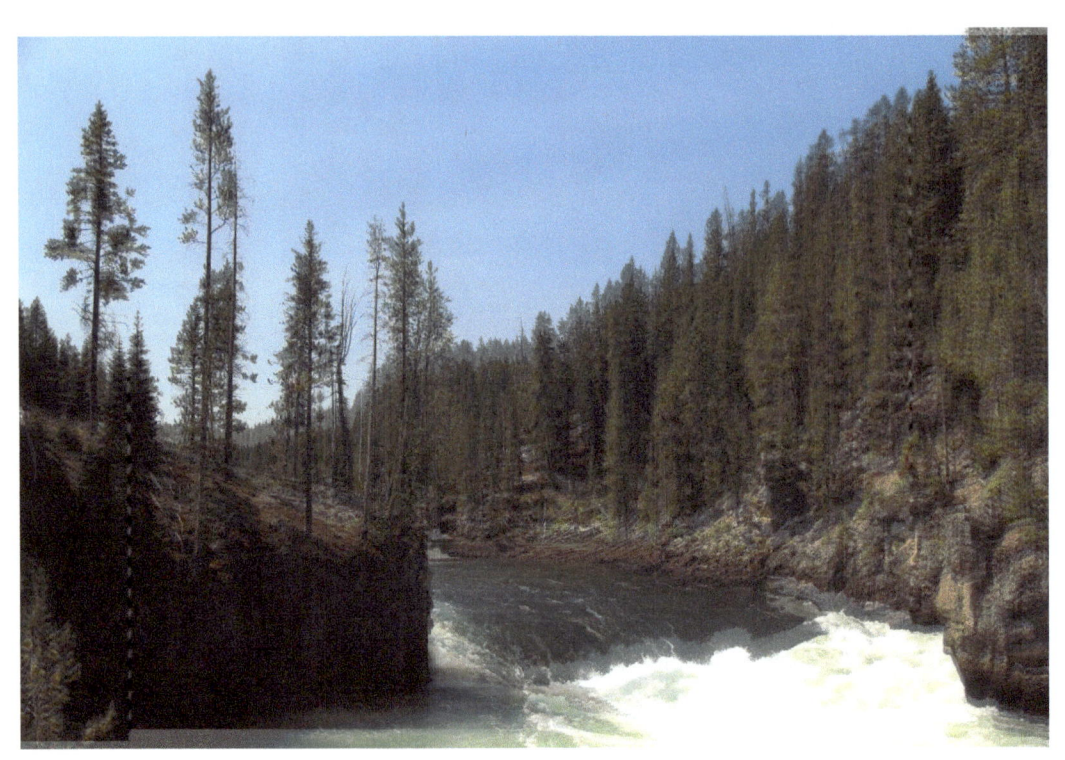

art ALL around
ART has the crown

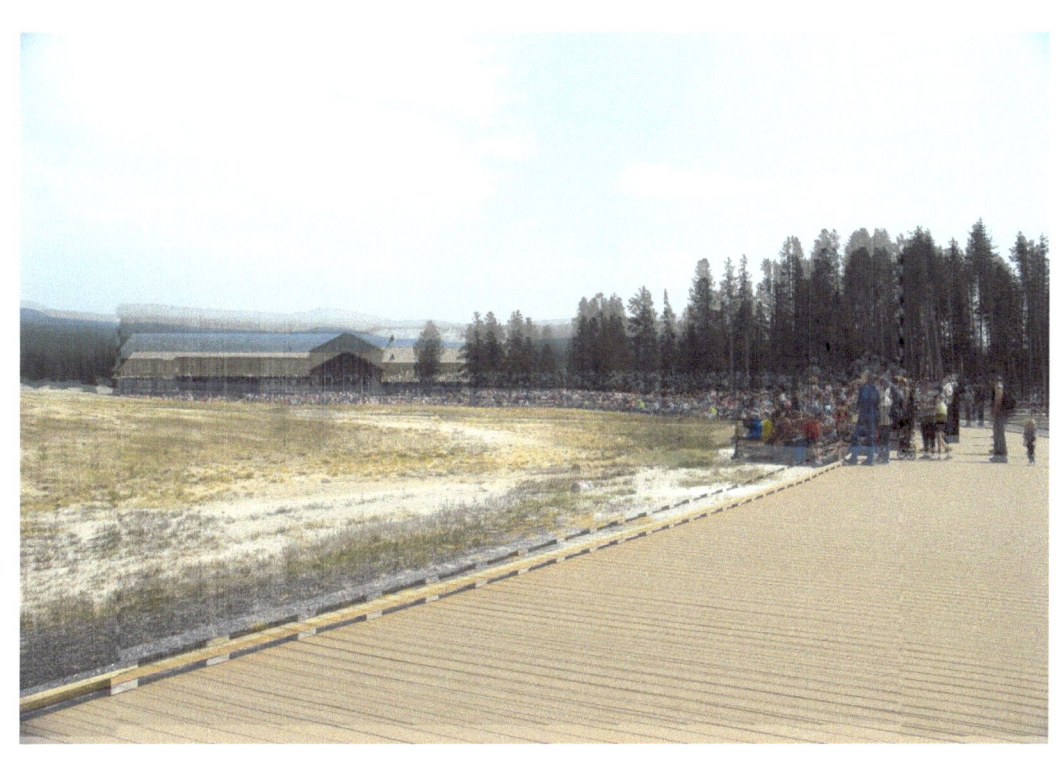

wyoming asked,
"AREN'T YOU GLAD YOU KNOW ME?"

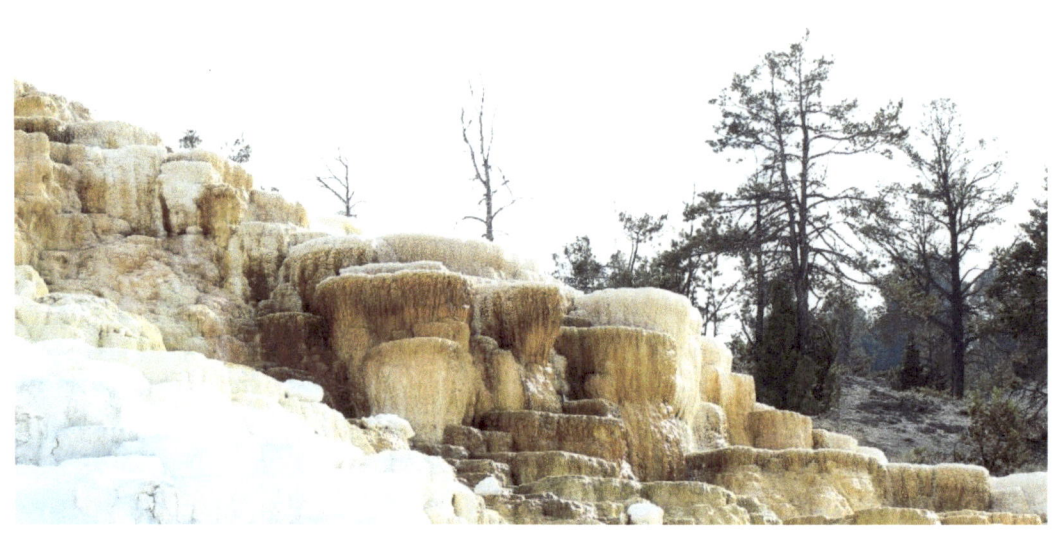

art ALL around
ART has the crown
edition 2

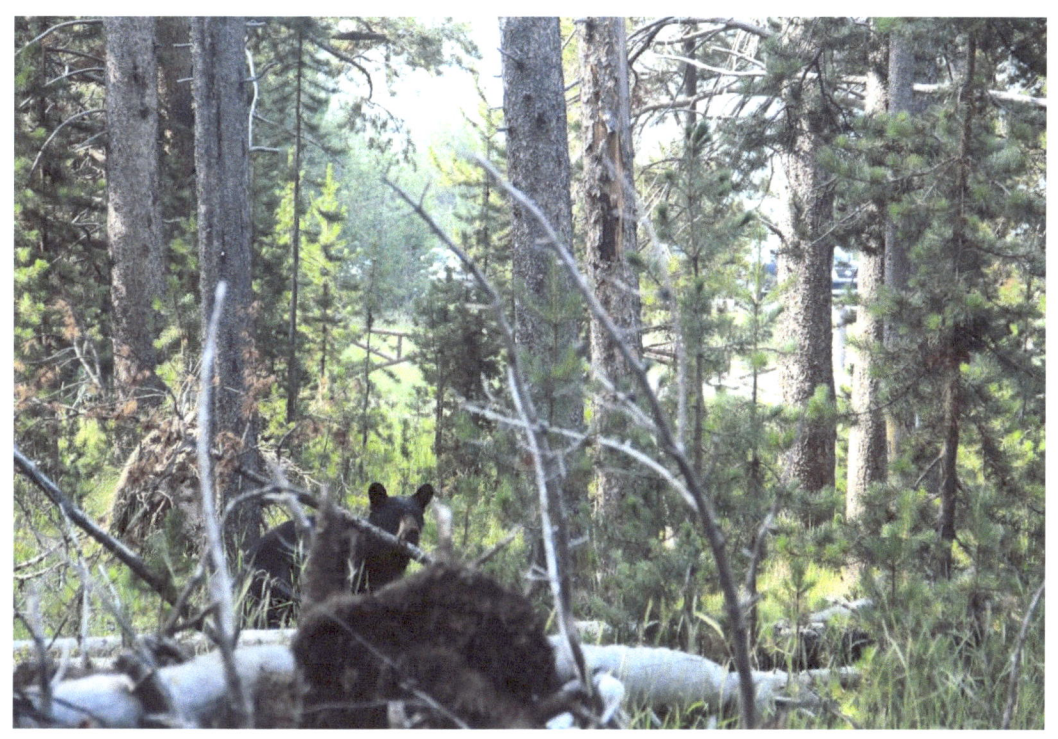

away from the california fence
WYOMING made SENSE
edition 2

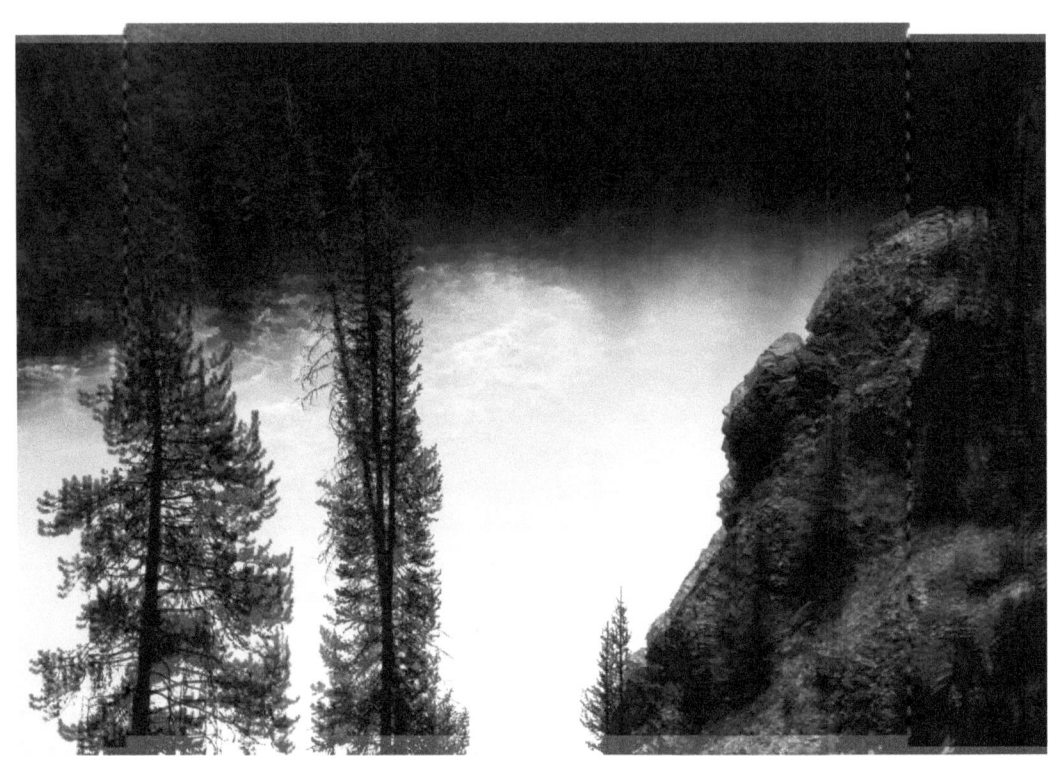

I want to be a l i v e through it all
i WANT to be alive with AWE
edition 2

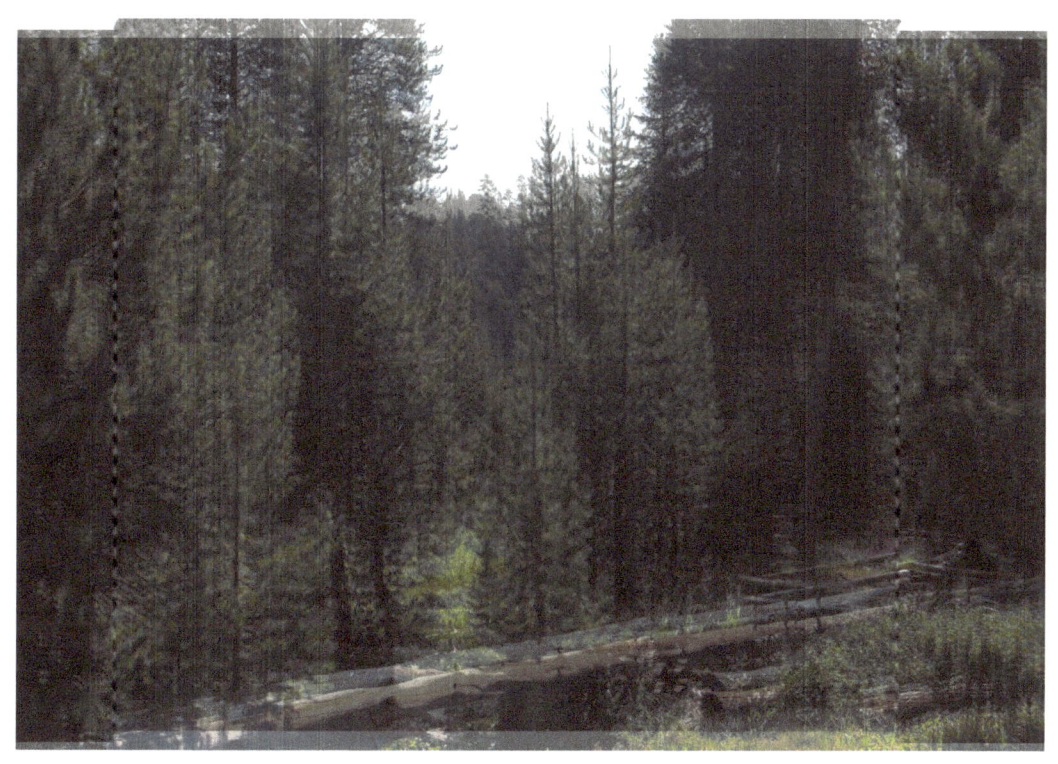

rage through the trenches you're in
YOU can WIN

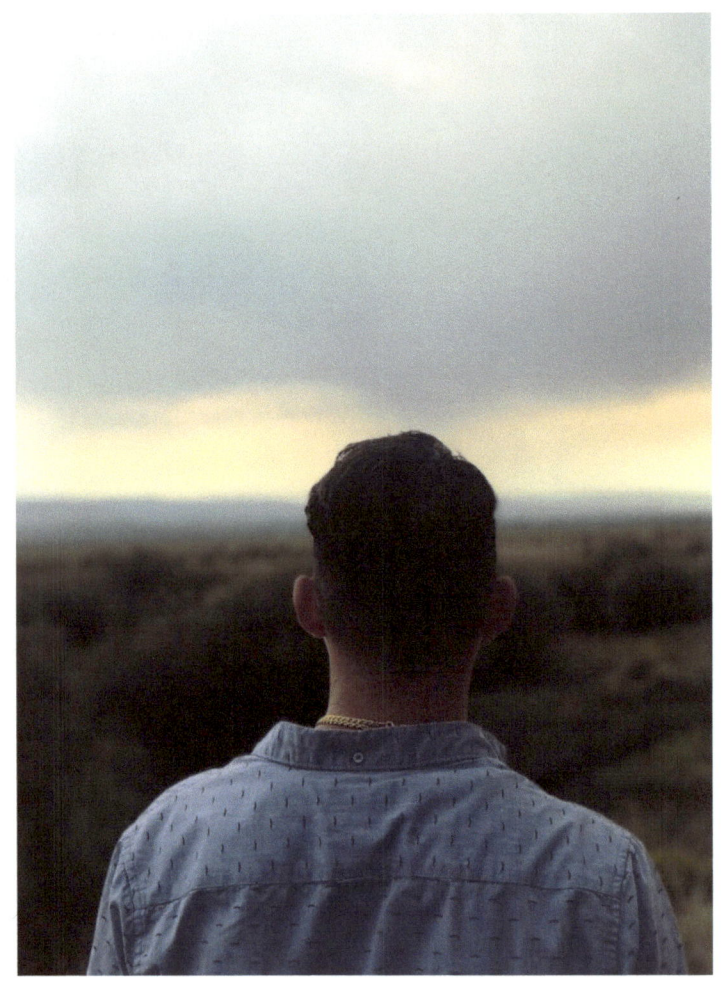

WYOMING, wyoming, your VIEWS heal
wyoming, wyoming, i'm glad you're real

THANK YOU
STAY CONFIDENT

www.ingramcontent.com/pod-product-compliance
Lightning Source LLC
Chambersburg PA
CBHW051945210526
45473CB00006B/2390